Sketchbook of Psalms

By

Jill Mockingbird

Hi! I hope you enjoy this cartoon sketchbook of the Bible. I hope it simplifies things for you & helps you understand. Since the covid quarantine at home, I've had a lot of time to put these sketches together. I hope it blesses you.

God is with you,
Jill

Hey! wait for me!

wicked

Blessed is the one who does not walk in step with the wicked.
Ps. 1:1

sinner's way

or stand in the way that sinners take
Ps. 1:2

ha ha!

or sit in the company of mockers.
Ps. 1:3

God's law

but whose delight is in the law of the Lord, and who meditates on his law day & night.

That person is like a tree planted by streams of water

which yields its fruit in season & whose leaf does not wither

prospers

righteous

whatever they do prospers. Ps. 1:3

He shall be like a tree
Planted by the rivers of water,
That brings forth its fruit in its season.
Psalms 1:3

Not so the wicked! They are like chaff that the wind blows away. Ps.1:4

Nor sinners in the assembly of the righteous

righteous

sinners

judgement
Therefore the wicked will not stand in the judgement.

For the Lord watches over the way of the righteous but

Lord

the way of the wicked leads to destruction

way of the wicked

destruction

way of the righteous

4

trust

Blessed are they
that put their trust
in the Lord.
Ps. 2

MY TRUST

Blessed are
all who take
refuge in Him
Ps. 2:12

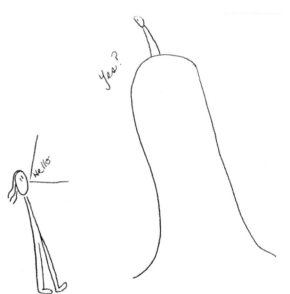

I cried to the Lord with my voice, And He heard me from His holy hill Psalms 3:4

I lay down and slept; I awoke, for the Lord sustained me. Psalms 3:5

the fire will test each one's work
of what sort it is   Ps. 3:18

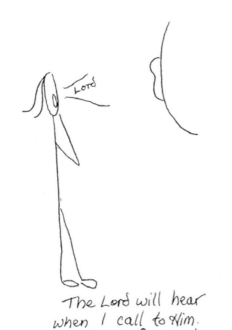

The Lord will hear
when I call to Him.
Psalms 4:3

Meditate within your heart
on your bed and be still.
Psalm 4:5

Wisdom is supreme; therefore get wisdom. Though it cost all you have, get understanding.
Ps. 4:7

Oh, save me for your mercies sake!
For in death there is no remembrance of you;
In the grave who will give you thanks?
Psalm 6:5

I am weary with my groaning.
All night I make my bed swim;
I drench my couch with my tears
... the Lord has heard my weeping.
The Lord will receive my prayer.
Psalm 6:6-9

My shield is
God most high.
Ps. 7:10

I will praise the Lord
according to His
righteousness,
And will sing praise to
the name of the Lord
Most High. Ps. 7:17

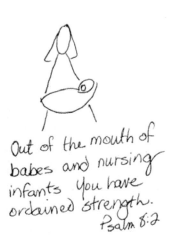

Out of the mouth of babes and nursing infants you have ordained strength.
Psalm 8:2

When I consider your heavens, the work of your fingers, The moon and stars, which you have ordained, what is man...?
Ps. 8:3

What is man that you are mindful of him, the son of man, that you care for him?
Ps. 8:4

When I consider your heaven, the
work of your fingers, the moon and the
stars, which you have set in place.
Ps. 8:7

The Lord is in His holy temple,
The Lord's throne is in heaven;
His eyes behold,
His eyelids test the sons of men.
Ps. 11:4

He who waters
will be watered
himself. Ps. 11:25

The words of the Lord
are pure words,
Like silver tried in a
furnace of earth,
Purified seven times.
Ps. 12:6

How long, O Lord?
Will you forget me forever?
How long will you hide
Your face from me?
Ps. 13:1

Lord, you alone are my portion and my cup. Ps.16:5

My body also will live in hope Ps.16:9

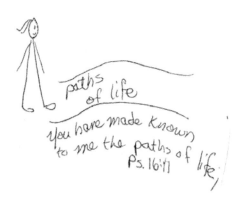

paths of life

you have made known to me the paths of life. Ps. 16:11

The boundary lines have fallen
for me in pleasant places;
surely I have a delightful
inheritance. Ps. 16:6

He drew me out of deep waters.
Ps. 18:16

The Lord was my support. He also brought me out into a broad place; He delivered me because He delighted in me.
Ps. 18:18-19

we'll get you out

He reached down from on high & took hold of me, he drew me out of deep waters Ps. 18:16

16

David   the Lord

You will show me the path of life; In your presence is fullness of joy.

I have set the Lord always before me; Because He is at my right hand I shall not be moved. Ps. 16:8-11

Keep me as the apple of your eye; Hide me under the shadow of your wings. Ps. 17:8

He reached down & took hold of me Ps. 18:16

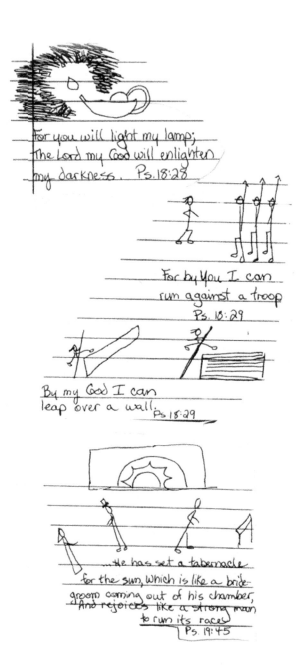

For you will light my lamp;
The Lord my God will enlighten
my darkness.   Ps. 18:28

For by You I can
run against a troop
Ps. 18:29

By my God I can
leap over a wall. Ps 18:29

...He has set a tabernacle
for the sun, Which is like a bride-
groom coming out of his chamber,
And rejoices like a strong man
to run its race
Ps. 19:4-5

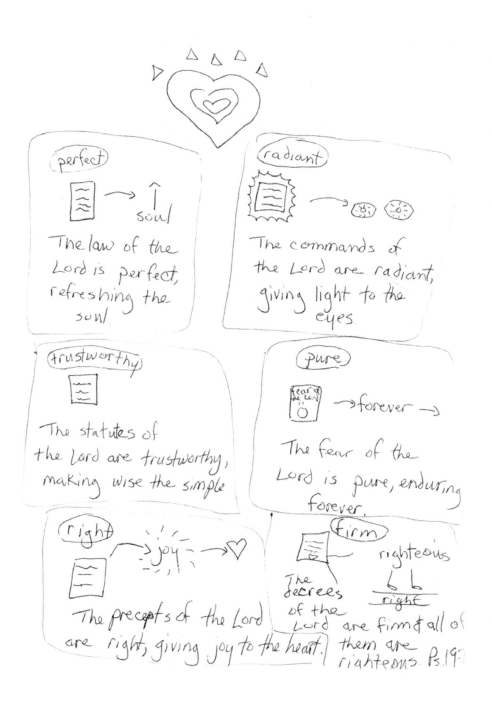

perfect

→ soul

The law of the Lord is perfect, refreshing the soul

radiant

The commands of the Lord are radiant, giving light to the eyes.

trustworthy

The statutes of the Lord are trustworthy, making wise the simple

pure

→ forever →

The fear of the Lord is pure, enduring forever.

right

→ joy → ♡

The precepts of the Lord are right, giving joy to the heart.

firm

righteous

right

The decrees of the Lord are firm & all of them are righteous. Ps.19

The Lord is my rock
Ps. 18:2

Let the words of my mouth & the meditation of my heart Be acceptable in your sight... Ps. 19:14

Some trust in chariots, and some in horses; But we will remember the name of the Lord our God. Ps. 20:7

the Lord our God

Ps. 22:12-16 Many bulls have surrounded me... They gape at me with their mouths... I am poured out like water... my heart is like wax. It has melted within me... dogs surround me.

Jesus!

I will declare your name to the brethren; In the midst of the assembly I will praise you

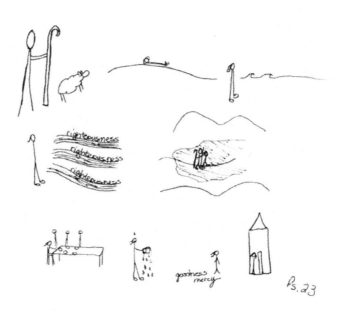

righteousness
righteousness
righteousness

goodness
mercy

Ps. 23

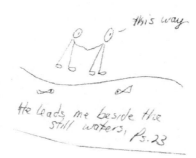

~this way

He leads me beside the
still waters, Ps. 23

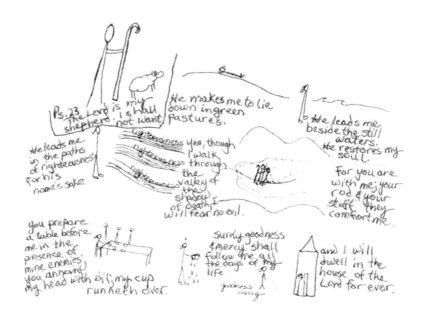

Ps. 23 The Lord is my shepherd; I shall not want. He makes me to lie down in green pastures.

He leads me in the paths of righteousness for his name's sake.

righteousness righteousness righteousness

Yea, though I walk through the valley of the shadow of death, I will fear no evil.

He leads me beside the still waters. He restores my soul.

For you are with me; your rod & your staff they comfort me.

You prepare a table before me in the presence of mine enemies; you anoint my head with oil; my cup runneth over.

Surely goodness & mercy shall follow me all the days of my life.

goodness mercy

and I will dwell in the house of the Lord for ever.

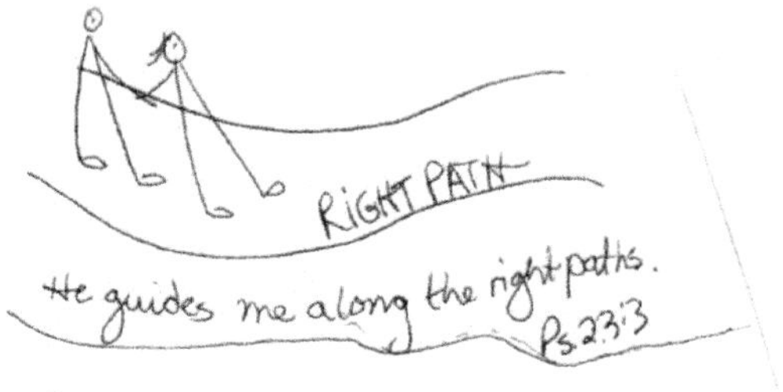

RIGHT PATH

He guides me along the right paths. Ps. 23:3

your goodness & love

Surely your goodness and love will follow me all the days of my life. Ps. 23:6

Goodness
mercy

January

HOUSE of
the Lord

Surely goodness
& mercy will
follow me all the
days of my life.

And I will dwell
in the house of
the Lord forever.
Ps. 23:6

for only He will
release my feet from
the snare. Ps 25:15

Goodness
mercy

Surely goodness
& mercy will
follow me all the
days of my life.

And I will dwell
in the house of
the Lord forever.
Ps. 23:6

For only He will
release my feet from
the snare. Ps 25:15

clean han..
pure heart

Holy
Place

Who may ascend
into the hill of the
Lord? Or who may
stand in this holy place
He who has clean hands
& a pure heart. Ps.24:8

Mercy   Truth

All the paths of the Lord
are mercy and truth.
Ps 25:10

Lord

My eyes are ever
toward the Lord,
For He shall pluck my
feet out of the net.
Ps. 25:15

One thing
have I
desired of
the Lord;
this only
do I seek
that I may
dwell in
the house of the Lord
all the days of my
life.
Ps. 27:4

He shall set me
high upon a rock.
Ps. 27:5

Hear the voice of my
supplications
when I cry to you,
when I lift my hands
toward your holy
sanctuary. Ps 28:2

The Lord is my
strength and
my shield Ps.28:7

Therefore my heart greatly
rejoices, And with my song
I will praise him Ps. 28:7

Weeping
may endure
for a night

But joy
comes in
the morning
Ps. 30:5

Ps 30:5 weeping may stay for the night, but rejoicing comes in the morning

When you hid your face, I was dismayed. Ps. 30 7

"You have turned for me my mourning into dancing; you have put off my sackcloth and clothed me with gladness. Ps. 30:11

you are my strength. Ps 31:45

into your hand I commit my spirit

You...have not
shut me up into the hand
of the enemy; You have set
my feet in a wide place.
Ps. 31:8

Surely in a flood of
great waters They shall
not come near him. You are
my hiding place; You shall
preserve me from trouble;
You shall surround me with
songs of deliverance Ps 32:6-7

Do not be like the horse or like
the mule, which have no understanding
Ps 32:9

Be strong &
take heart you
who hope in
the Lord. Ps.31:24

Be of good courage
& He shall strengthen
your heart. Ps.31:24

I will guide you
with my eye. Ps.32:8

Go this way

I will instruct you
and teach you in
the way you should
go Ps.32:8

go this way

Shout for joy,
all you upright
in heart.
Ps. 32:11

Happy are the people
whose God is the Lord!
Ps. 33:12

fear &
awe

Let all the earth fear
the Lord; Let all the
inhabitants of the world
stand in awe of Him
Ps. 33:8

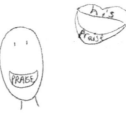

I will bless the Lord
at all times; His praise
shall continually be in
my mouth.   Ps. 34:1

Fears

I sought the Lord, and He
heard me and delivered me
from all my fears. Ps 34:4

This poor man cried out, and
the Lord heard Him. And saved
him out of all his troubles.
Ps. 34:6

The angel of the Lord
encamps all around those
who fear Him, And delivers
them   Ps. 34:7

35

Oh magnify the Lord with me, And let us exalt His name together Ps 34.3

-Where's God?

Here I am!

I sought the Lord, & He heard me, And delivered me from all my sins Ps. 34:4

righteous

for the eyes of the Lord are on the righteous Ps. 34:15

O taste and see that the Lord is good. Ps 34:8

Ps. 34:13 Keep your tongue from evil & your lips from speaking deceit

Do not fret because of evildoers, Nor be envious of the workers of iniquity. For they shall soon be cut down like the grass, And wither as the green herb. Ps. 37:1-2

God's way

Commit your way to the Lord, Trust also in Him And He shall bring it to pass. Ps 37:5

But the face of the Lord is against those who do evil. Ps. 34:16

The Lord is near to those who have a contrite heart, And saves such as have a contrite spirit. Ps 34:18

They reward me evil for good, To the sorrow of my soul. Ps. 35:12

righteousness

faithfulness

mercy

Your mercy, O Lord, is in the heavens; your faithfulness reaches the clouds. Your righteousness is like the great mountains. Ps. 36:5-6

He shall bring forth
your righteousness as
the light, And your justice
as the noonday. Ps 37:6

LORD

Rest in the Lord, and
wait patiently for Him
Ps. 37:7

Meek

But the meek shall
inherit the earth
Ps 3:

This is
for you!

BLESSED

I have been
young, and now
am old; Yet I
have not seen
the righteous

righteous

forsaken...He is ever merciful and lends;
And his descendents are blessed. Ps37:
25;

Go here..
Now go here
The steps of a good man are ordered by the Lord.
Ps. 37:23
Go this way!
Though he fall, he shall not be utterly cast down; for the Lord upholds him with His hand. Ps. 37:24

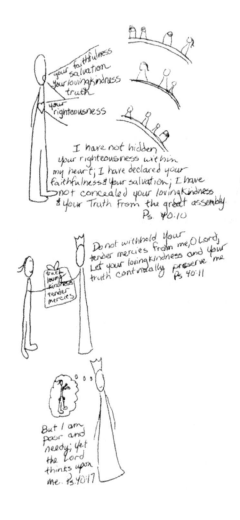

your faithfulness
your salvation
your lovingkindness
truth
your righteousness

I have not hidden
your righteousness within
my heart; I have declared your
faithfulness & your salvation; I have
not concealed your lovingkindness
& your Truth From the great assembly.
Ps. 40:10

Do not withhold Your
tender mercies from me, O Lord;
Let your lovingkindness and your
truth continually preserve me.
Ps 40:11

truth
lovingkindness
tender mercies

But I am
poor and
needy; yet
the Lord
thinks upon
me. Ps. 40:17

42

kindness

The Lord will command His lovingkindness in the daytime, And in the night His song shall be with me—
Ps. 42:8

why are you cast down, O my soul? And why are you disquieted within me?

Hope in God; For I shall yet praise Him, The help of my countenance & my God.
Ps. 42:11

He will be my guide even to death Ps. 48:14

Let your loving
kindness and
truth continually
preserve me.
Ps. 40:11

thank
you

Here. Have
some bread

Even my close friend,
someone I trusted,
one who shared my bread,
has turned against me.
Ps. 41:8

at night, his song
is with me.   Ps. 42:8

In God we boast
all day long,
And praise your
name forever. Ps. 44:8

My tongue is
the pen of a
ready writer. Ps. 45:1

God
God
God

God
God
God

In God
we boast
all day
long
And praise
your name
forever
Ps. 44:8

God is our refuge & strength. A very present help in trouble. Therefore we will not fear

Even though the earth be removed, And though the mountains be carried into the midst of the sea; Though its waters roar and be troubled, Though the mountains shake with its swelling.

There is a river whose streams shall make glad the City of God. Ps 46:1-4

no
fear

Therefore we will not fear, though the earth give way & the mountains fall into the heart of the sea.

Ps. 46:2

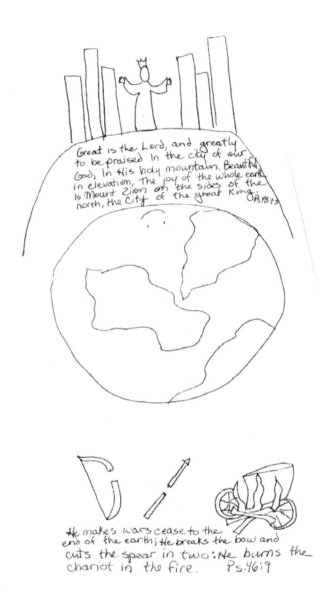

Great is the Lord, and greatly to be praised In the city of our God, In His holy mountain. Beautiful in elevation, The joy of the whole earth Is Mount Zion on the sides of the north, the City of the great King. Ps.48:1-3

He makes wars cease to the end of the earth; He breaks the bow and cuts the spear in two; He burns the chariot in the fire.   Ps.46:9

A broken and a contrite
heart - these, O God, you
will not despise ... He
heals the broken hearted
and binds up their wounds
Ps 51:17

friend

It is not an enemy who reproaches
me; Then I could bear it ... But it
was you, a man my equal, my
companion. and my acquaintance
Ps. 55:12-13

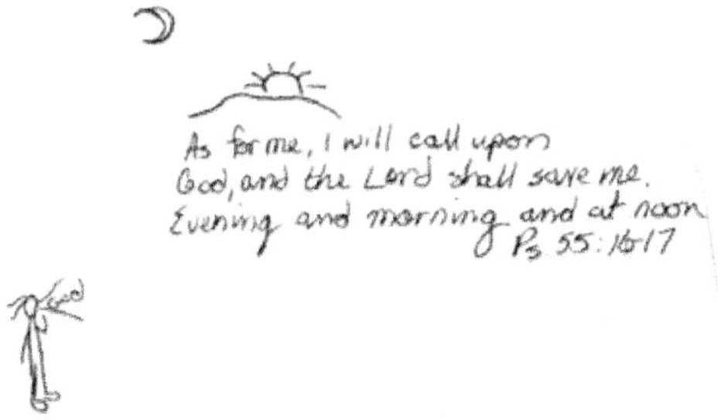
As for me, I will call upon
God, and the Lord shall save me.
Evening and morning and at noon
Ps. 55:16-17

This is too much! Thank you.
burden
You're welcome.
I got this.

cast your burden on the Lord and He shall sustain you.
Ps. 55:22

In God I have
put my trust; I will
not fear. What can flesh
do to me? Ps 56:4

calamities

And in the shadow of Your
wings I will make your
refuge, Until these calamities
have passed by. Ps. 57:1

your
power
your
mercy

I will sing of your power;
Yes, I will sing aloud of your
mercy in the morning,
Ps. 59:16

51

GOD

mercy

truth

Glory

For your mercy reaches
unto the heavens,
And your truth unto the clouds
Be exalted, O God, above the
heavens; Let your glory be above
all the earth   Ps. 57/0

O God!

From the end of the
earth I will cry to
you.   Ps 61 2

For it is He who
shall tread down
our enemies
Ps 60:12

when my heart is
overwhelmed; Lead me
to the rock that is
higher than I.   Ps. 61:2

BLESSINGS

curse

They bless with
their mouth,
But they curse
inwardly Ps. 62:4

Pour out
your heart
before Him
Ps 62:8

If riches increase,
do not set your
heart on them
Ps 62:10

My flesh longs for you in a dry & thirsty
land where there is no water.

Ps 63:1

My lips shall
praise You Thus
will I bless You
while I live.
Ps. 63:3

You visit the earth and water it Ps 65:9

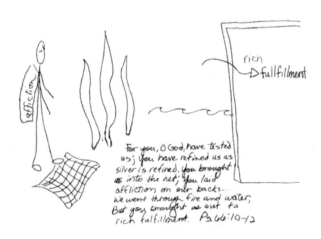

affliction

rich
→ fullfillment

For you, O God, have tested
us; you have refined us as
silver is refined. you brought
us into the net; you laid
affliction on our backs...
we went through fire and water;
But you brought us out to
rich fulfillment. Ps 66:10-12

Blessed be
the Lord who
daily loads us
with benefits.
Ps 68:19

Praise be to
God, who daily
bears our
burdens
Ps 68:19

God be merciful
to us & bless us,
& cause His face
to shine upon us
Ps. 67:1

O my prayer → thank you

← mercy

Blessed be God,
Who has not turned
away my prayer, Nor
His mercy from me
Ps. 68:20

A father of the fatherless...
Is God in His holy habitation. Ps. 68:5

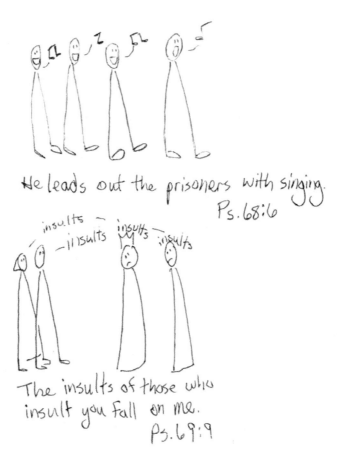

He leads out the prisoners with singing.
Ps. 68:6

The insults of those who
insult you fall on me.
Ps. 69:9

God sets the solitary
in families
Ps 68:6

Blessed be the Lord
who daily loads us
with benefits
Ps. 68:19

But I am poor an
sorrowful; Let you
salvation, O God, set m
up on high. I will
praise the name of
God with a song.
Ps 69:29-30

Deliver me out of the mire,
And let me not sink; Let me
be delivered from those who
hate me, And out of the deep
waters. Let not the floodwaters
overflow me Ps 69: 14-15

Let heaven and earth
praise Him, The seas
and everything that moves
in them. Ps 69:34

PRAISE

Let heaven and earth
praise Him, The seas
and everything that
moves in them
        Ps 69:34

let those who love
your salvation say
continually "Let God
be magnified"
Ps. 70:4

on the harp
I will praise
you

He shall come down like
rain upon the grass before
mowing, Like showers that
water the earth.
Ps. 72:6

I have become a stranger to
my brothers, And an alien to
my mother's children; Because
zeal for your house has eaten
me up   Ps. 69. 8-9

Save me, O God!
for the waters come up
to my neck. I sink in
deep mire, where there
is no standing; I have
come into deep waters
where the floods overflow
me. I am weary with
crying; My throat is dry
My eyes fail while I wait
for my God.   Ps. 69

may the
mountains
bring
prosperity
to the people
—Ps 72:3

the hills
the fruit
of righteousness

Ps. 73:26
My flesh and
my heart may
fail, but God is
the strength of my
heart and my portion forever.

You hold me by my
right hand. Ps. 73:25

You hold my
eyelids open Ps. 77:4

wickedness

I would rather be a
doorkeeper in the house of
my God than dwell in the
tents of wickedness.
Ps. 84:10

Sing aloud to God our
strength; Make a joyful
shout to the God of Jacob.
Raise a song and strike the timbrel,
The pleasant harp with the lute.
Blow the trumpet at the time of the
New Moon   Ps. 81:1-3

Open your mouth
wide, and I will
fill it   Ps. 81:10

He would have
fed them also with
the finest of wheat;
And with honey from
the rock, I would have
satisfied you. Ps. 81:16

My heart & flesh
cry out for the
living God. Ps. 84:2

thank
you

No good thing will He
withhold from those who
walk uprightly. Ps.84:11

You have fed
them with the bread
of tears

And given them tears
in great measure.
Ps. 80:5

nice to meet

 mercy truth

 righteousness peace

 truth

Mercy and truth
have met together

Righteousness
and peace
have kissed

Truth shall
spring out of
the earth,

And righteousness shall look
down from heaven.
Ps. 85:10-11

WRATH

Terrors

Your fierce wrath has
gone over me; your
terrors have cut me off.
They came around me all
day like water. Ps. 88:16-17

Praise
the Lord

Will you work wonders
for the dead? Shall the
dead arise and praise you?
Ps. 88:10

mercies mercies mercies

I will sing of the mercies
of the Lord forever
Ps. 89:1

God's faithfulness

with my mouth will I make
known Your faithfulness to
all generations.   Ps. 89:1

Beauty

Let the beauty of
the Lord our God be
upon us, And establish
the work of our hand
Ps. 90:17

The righteous shall flourish
like a palm tree, he shall grow
like a cedar in Lebanon.
Ps. 92:12

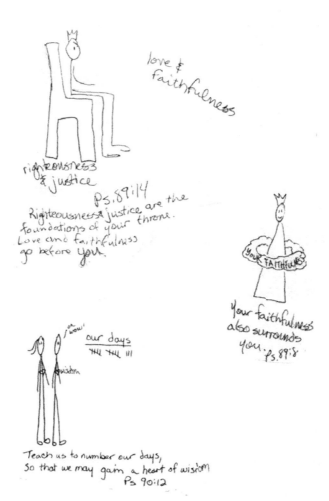

love &
faithfulness

righteousness
& justice

Ps. 89:14
Righteousness & justice are the
foundations of your throne.
Love and faithfulness
go before you.

Your FAITHFULNESS

Your faithfulness
also surrounds
you. Ps. 89:8

'oh!
wow!'
our days
卌 卌 ⫶⫶⫶

wisdom

Teach us to number our days,
so that we may gain a heart of wisdom
Ps 90:12

He who dwells in the secret
place of the Most High
Shall abide under the
shadow of the Almighty.
Ps.91:1

I will say of the Lord, "He is
my refuge and my fortress;
My God, in Him will I trust."
Ps. 91:2

You shall not be afraid of the terror
by night; Nor of the arrow that flies by day,
Nor of the pestilence that walks in
darkness; Nor of the destruction that
lays waste at noonday. Ps.91:5-6

A thousand may fall
at your side, And ten
thousand at your right
hand; But it shall not
come near you. Only with
your eyes shall you look
Ps. 91:7-8

You shall tread upon the lion and the cobra. The young lion and the serpent you shall trample underfoot. Ps. 91:13

Their righteous shall flourish like a palm tree, Those who are planted in the house of the Lord Ps. 92:12

He shall grow like a cedar Lebanon.

your lovingkindness

your faithfulness

It is good to give thanks to the Lord...
To declare your lovingkindness in the morning,
And your faithfulness at night Ps. 92:1-2

The floods have lifted up, O Lord,
The floods have lifted up their voice;
The floods lift up their waves.

The Lord on high is mightier
Than the noise of many waters,
Than the mighty waves of the sea.
Ps 93:3-4

He who planted the ear, shall
He not hear?
He who planted the eye, shall
He not see?   Ps 94:9

In His hand are the
deep places of the earth;
The heights of the hills are His, also
The sea is His, for He made it;
And His hands formed the
dry land.   Ps 95:4-5

His voice   yes?

Today, if you hear His voice:
'Do not harden your hearts....
Ps 95:7-8

mercy

"my foot slips"

If I say "my foot
slips," Your mercy,
O Lord, will hold me up
Ps 94:18

72

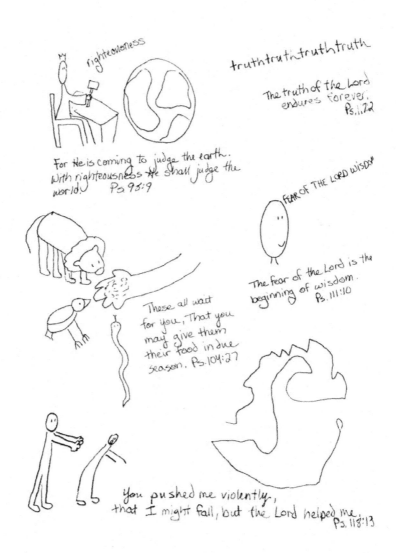

righteousness

For He is coming to judge the earth. With righteousness He shall judge the world. Ps 96:9

truthtruthtruthtruth

The truth of the Lord endures forever. Ps. 117:2

These all wait for you, That you may give them their food in due season. Ps. 104:27

FEAR OF THE LORD WISDOM

The fear of the Lord is the beginning of wisdom. Ps. 111:10

You pushed me violently, that I might fall, but the Lord helped me. Ps. 118:13

Sing to the Lord,
all the earth.
Ps 96:1

Give to
the Lord
glory &
strength.
Ps 96:7

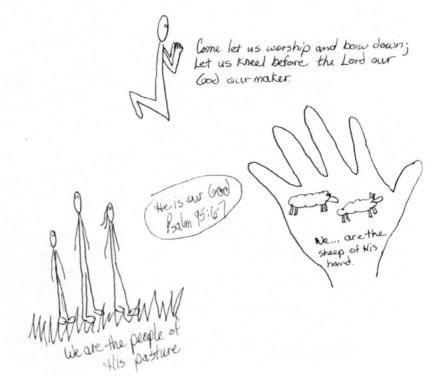

Come let us worship and bow down;
Let us kneel before the Lord our
God our maker.

He is our God
Psalm 95:6-7

We.... are the
sheep of His
hand.

We are the people of
His pasture

Let the heavens Rejoice!

and let the earth be Glad

R o a r
→ let the sea roar, and all its fullness

Let the field be joyful

Then all the trees of the woods will rejoice before the Lord.

For He is coming ...
Ps. 96:11-13

Mercy ——→
truth ——→

you goo
ga ga

His mercy is everlasting,
And His truth endures to
all generations. Ps. 100:5

Exalt

Exalt the Lord our
God, And worship
at His holy hill; for the
Lord our God is holy.
Ps. 99:9

thanksgiving
praise

Enter into His gates with
thanksgiving and into His courts
with praise. Ps. 100:4

Make a joyful shout to the Lord,
all you lands! Ps.100:1

I will walk within
my house with a perfect
heart. Ps. 101:2

Whoever secretly
slanders his
neighbor, Him I
will destroy; The
one who Has a
haughty look and
a proud heart,
Him I will not endure
Ps. 101:5

WICKED

I will set nothing wicked before my eyes.
Ps. 101:3

I am like a pelican
of the wilderness;
I am like an owl of
the desert.
I lie awake, And
am like a sparrow
alone on the housetop.
Ps. 102:6-7

Let this be written
for a future generation
that a people not yet
created may serve
the Lord Ps. 102:18

yes?

He shall regard the prayer of
the destitute, And shall not despise
their prayer. Ps. 102:17

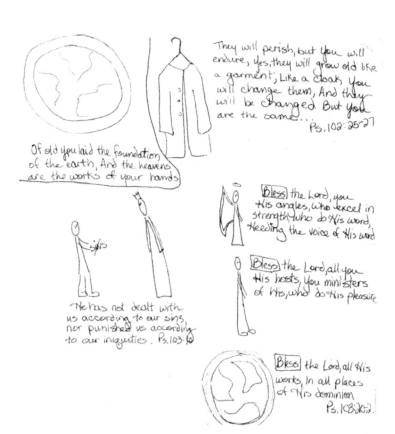

They will perish, but you will endure; Yes, they will grow old like a garment; Like a cloak You will change them, And they will be changed. But you are the same...
Ps. 102:25-27

Of old you laid the foundation of the earth, And the heavens are the works of your hands

sins

He has not dealt with us according to our sins, nor punished us according to our iniquities. Ps. 103:10

Bless the Lord, you His angles, who excel in strength, who do His word, Heeding the voice of His word

Bless the Lord, all you His hosts, You ministers of His, who do His pleasure

Bless the Lord, all His works, In all places of His dominion
Ps. 103:20-22

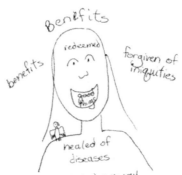

Benefits

benefits

redeemed

forgiven of iniquities

good things

healed of diseases

Bless the Lord, O my soul,
And forget not all His benefits;
Who forgives all your iniquities,
Who heals all your diseases,
Who redeems your life from
destruction, who crowns
you with lovingkindness & tender mercy;
Who satisfies your mouth with
good things, so that your
youth is renewed like the eagles
Ps 103:1-5

I will sing to the Lord as long as I live;
I will sing praise to my God while I have
my being. Ps. 104:33

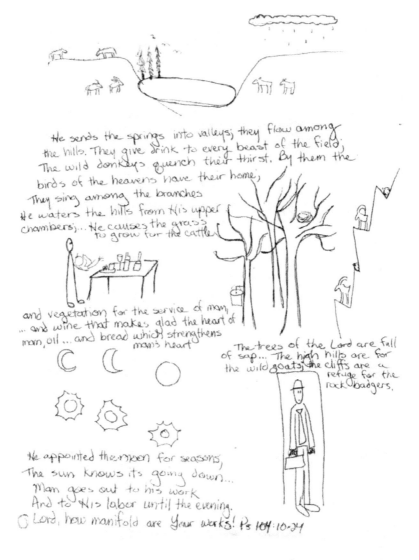

He sends the springs into valleys; they flow among the hills. They give drink to every beast of the field; The wild donkeys quench their thirst. By them the birds of the heavens have their home; They sing among the branches He waters the hills from His upper chambers;... He causes the grass to grow for the cattle,

and vegetation for the service of man, ... and wine that makes glad the heart of man, oil ... and bread which strengthens man's heart

The trees of the Lord are full of sap... The high hills are for the wild goats; the cliffs are a refuge for the rock badgers.

He appointed the moon for seasons; The sun knows its going down... Man goes out to his work And to His labor until the evening. O Lord, how manifold are Your works! Ps 104:10-24

he stretches out the
heavens like a tent. Ps 104:2

But our God is in heaven. He does what He pleases. Their idols are silver and gold, The work of men's hands. They have mouths, but they do not speak; Eyes they have, but they do not see. They have ears, but they do

Ps. 108:1-3 O God, my heart is steadfast; I will sing and give praise ... Awake, lute and harp! I will awaken the dawn. I will praise You O Lord

not hear; Noses they have, but they do not smell; They have hands, but they do not handle; Feet they have, but they do not walk; Nor do they mutter through their throat. Those who make them are like them. Ps. 115:

But I give myself to prayer. Ps. 109:4

He grants the barren woman a home - Like a joyful mother of children. Ps. 113:9

83

I called on the Lord
in distress; The Lord
answered me and set me
in a broad place. Ps.118:5

righteous
go through
here

The Lord is on my side.
I will not fear. What can
man do to me? Ps.118:6

from the
rising of the
sun

to its
going down

the name of the
Lord is to be praised.
Ps.113:3

Open to me the gates of
righteousness; I will go
through them, And I will
praise the Lord. This is the
gate of the Lord, Through
which the righteous will enter.
                        Ps 117:19-20

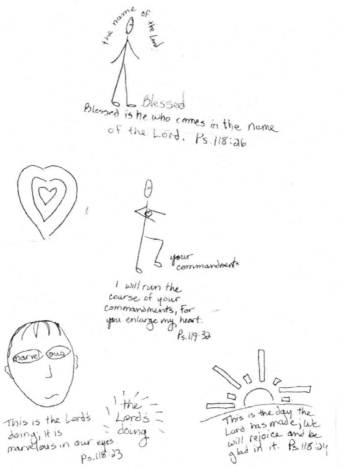

the name of the Lord

Blessed

Blessed is he who comes in the name of the Lord. Ps. 118:26

your commandments

I will run the course of your commandments, for you enlarge my heart.
Ps. 119:32

marvel ous

This is the Lord's doing; It is marvelous in our eyes
Ps. 118:23

the Lord's doing

This is the day the Lord has made; we will rejoice and be glad in it. Ps. 118:24

proud

Though the Lord is on high,
Yet He regards the lowly;
But the proud He knows
from afar. Ps.138:6

God

trouble

trouble

trouble

wrath

STOP

Though I walk in the midst of trouble,
You will revive me; You will stretch
out Your hand Against the wrath of
my enemies, And Your right hand will save me.
Ps. 138:7

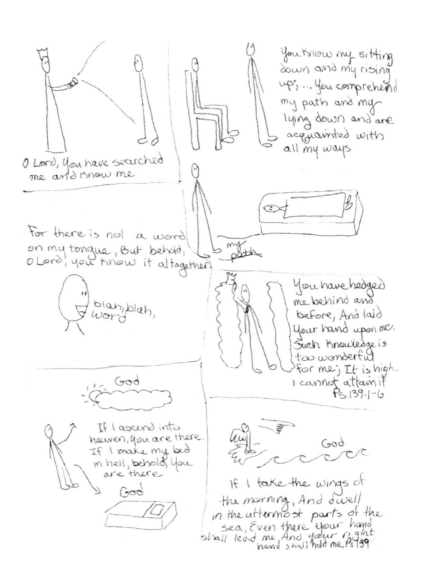

O Lord, You have searched me and know me

You know my sitting down and my rising up; ... You comprehend my path and my lying down and are acquainted with all my ways

For there is not a word on my tongue, But behold, O Lord, you know it altogether

blah, blah, word

You have hedged me behind and before, And laid Your hand upon me. Such knowledge is too wonderful for me; It is high, I cannot attain it Ps. 139.1-6

God

If I ascend into heaven, you are there. If I make my bed in hell, behold, You are there

God

God

If I take the wings of the morning, And dwell in the uttermost parts of the sea, Even there your hand shall lead me, And your right hand shall hold me, Ps 139

Set a guard over my
mouth; keep watch
over the door of my lips.
Ps 141:3

water
I please

I spread out my hands to you;
My soul longs for you like a thirsty land.
Ps.143:6

Happy are the people
whose God is the Lord!
Ps.144:15

Let his faithful
people ... sing for
joy on their beds.
Ps.149:5

Let the righteous strike me;
It shall be a kindness,
And let him rebuke me;
It shall be as excellent oil;
Let my head not refuse it.
Ps.141:5

I will sing a new
song to you, O, God;
On a harp of ten
strings I will sing
praises to you.
Ps.144:9

Have all the workers of iniquity no knowledge, who eat up my people as they eat bread? Ps. 114:4

your word

my ways

How can a young man cleanse his ways, by taking heed according to your word. Ps. 119:9

go this way

go this way

your words

Direct my steps by your words Ps. 119:13

Precious in the sight of the Lord
Is the death of His saints.
Prov. 116:15

I love the Lord
   because He has heard
   my voice and my supplications.
Because He has inclined His
ear to me, therefore I will call
upon Him as long as I live. Ps. 116:1

prosperity

O Lord, I pray,
send now prosperity
Ps. 118:25

Ps. 118:23
This was the Lord's doing & it
is marvelous in our eyes

Streams of tears flow
from my eyes,
for your law is
not obeyed.
Ps. 119:136

your
word

Your word is a
lamp unto my feet
Ps 119:105

your word

The entrance of
your words give
light. Ps 119:130

94

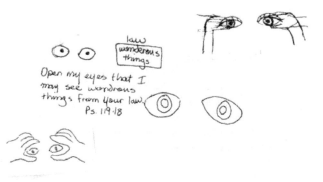

law
wonderous things

Open my eyes that I
may see wondrous
things from Your law.
Ps. 119:18

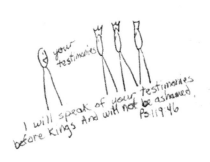

your testimonies

I will speak of your testimonies
before Kings And will not be ashamed.
Ps 119:46

your words

How sweet are your
words to my taste,
sweeter than
honey. Ps 119:103

your words

YOUR WORD HAS
GIVEN ME LIFE Ps.119:50

your testimonies... are the
rejoicing of my heart.
Ps.119:111

The entrance of Your
words gives light Ps.119:
130

your
words

I am for peace, but when I speak, they are for war. Ps. 120:7

The sun shall not strike you by day nor the moon by night. Ps 121:6

IN   OUT

The Lord shall preserve you from all evil; He shall preserve your soul. The Lord shall preserve your going out & your coming in. Ps 121:8

EXIT

ENTRANCE

I will lift up my eyes
to the hills-
From whence comes my help?
My help comes from the Lord,
Who made heaven & earth

Lord

I will lift up my
eyes to the hills-
from whence comes
my help? Ps.121:1-2

help

I will lift up my eyes to
the hills-
From whence comes my
help? My help comes
from the Lord, who made
heaven and earth.
Ps. 121:1

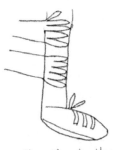

He will not allow your foot to be moved;
He who keeps you will not slumber. Ps. 121:3

He will not allow your foot to be moved.

As the eyes of the servants look to the hand of their masters, as the eyes of a maid to the hand of her mistress, so our eyes look to the Lord our God, until He has mercy on us. Ps. 123:2

mercy

Those who sow in tears
Shall reap in joy.
He who continually goes forth weeping,
Bearing seed for sowing,
Shall doubtless come again with rejoicing,
Bringing his sheaves with him.
                                        Ps. 126:5-6

Joy

As the mountains
surround Jerusalem,
so the Lord surrounds
His people from this
time and Forever.
Ps. 125:2

Those
who trust in
the Lord Are
like Mount Zion,
Which cannot be moved,
but abides forever.
Ps. 125:1

Lord's house

man's house

Unless the Lord builds the house,
They labor in vain who build it,
Ps. 127:1

given by God

children are a heritage
from the Lord. Ps 127:3

Like arrows in the hand
of a warrior, So are
the children of one's
youth. Happy is the man
who has his quiver full
of them.   Ps. 127:3-5

They shall not be ashamed,
But shall speak with their
enemies in the gate.
Ps. 127:5

Ps. 128:3-4 Your wife shall be like a
fruitful vine In the very
heart of your house, Your
children like olive plants
All around your table,... thus
shall the man be blessed who fears the Lord

the Lord

My soul waits for the Lord
More than those who watch
for the morning -Yes, more than
those who watch for the morning.
Ps. 130:6

Behold how good
and pleasant it is
for brethren to dwell
together in unity!
Ps. 133:1

It is like precious oil upon
the head, Running down on
the beard...Running down on
the edge of his garments
Ps. 133:2

Behold, bless
the Lord...who by
night stand in the
house of the Lord!
Lift up your hands
in the sanctuary
Ps. 134:1-2

house
of the
Lord

Do it!

His word

He sends out His command to the earth; His word runs very swiftly. He gives snow like wool; He scatters the frost like ashes; He casts out His hail like morsels; Who can stand before His cold? He sends out His word and melts them; He causes His wind to blow, and the waters flow. Ps. 147:15-18

"(..) brr"

Let the saints be joyful in glory.; Let them sing aloud on their beds. Let the high praises of God be in their mouth,

And a two edged sword in their hand.

Ps. 149:5-6

Praise Him with the sound of the trumpet Praise Him with the lute and harp! Praise Him with stringed instrument and flutes! Praise Him with loud cymbals.
Ps. 150:3-5

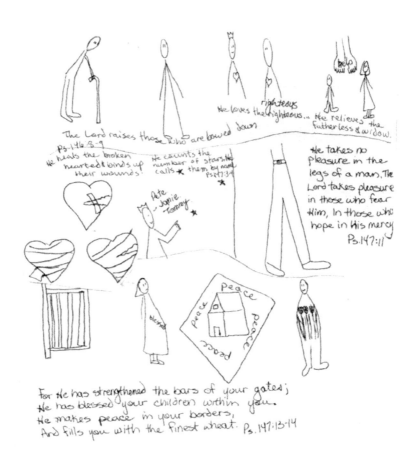

The Lord raises those who are bowed down
Ps. 146:8-9

He heals the broken hearted & binds up their wounds!

He counts the number of stars: He calls ★ them by name
Ps 147:3-4

He loves the righteous... He relieves the fatherless & widow.

help

He takes no pleasure in the legs of a man. The Lord takes pleasure in those who fear Him, In those who hope in His mercy
Ps. 147:11

Pete
Jamie
Tommy ★

blessed

peace peace peace peace peace

For He has strengthened the bars of your gates;
He has blessed your children within you.
He makes peace in your borders,
And fills you with the finest wheat. Ps. 147:13-14

gracious

great in mercy

slow to anger

compassion

tender mercies

God!

mercy

Ps. 145:8-9
The Lord is gracious and full of
compassion, Slow to anger and
great in mercy. The Lord is good to
all, And His tender mercies are over
all His works.

The Lord is near to
all who call upon
Him, To all who call
upon Him in truth
Ps. 145:18

Happy is he who
has the God of Jacob
for his help... whose hope is in the Lord who made heaven and earth, the sea and all that
is in them, who keeps truth forever, who executes justice for
the oppressed,
and all that

L°O°R°D°E

truth truth truth truth

I'm free!

I can see!

who gives food to the hungry. The Lord gives freedom to the prisoners. The Lord opens
the eyes of the blind... But the way of the wicked He turns upside down. Ps. 146:5-9